THIN THIGHS IN 30 DAYS

- *THE WORK-OFF*
- *THE WALK-OFF*
- *THE WEIGHT-OFF*

By Wendy Stehling

PHOTOS BY JOHN OLSON

DESIGNED BY LOUIS FALCONE

Congratulations on taking the first step towards a prettier and healthier you. This book is dedicated to all my readers. You're beautiful!

THIN THIGHS IN 30 DAYS
A Bantam Book / May 1982

All rights reserved.
Copyright © 1982 by Wendy Stehling.

ISBN 0-553-01443-9

Published simultaneously in the United States and Canada

Bantam Books are published by Bantam Books, Inc. Its trademark, consisting of the words "Bantam Books" and the portrayal of a rooster is Registered in U.S. Patent and Trademark Office and in other countries. Marca Registrada. Bantam Books, Inc., 666 Fifth Avenue, New York, New York 10103.

PRINTED IN THE UNITED STATES OF AMERICA

30   29   28   27   26   25

TABLE OF CONTENTS

"After 30 days, my reward is a fabulous evening at Regines!"

DRESS BY STEPHEN BURROWS/HENRI BEND
STYLED BY CHARLENE PERITO
HAIR AND MAKE UP RICK CALDWELL

INTRODUCTION

There they were in the department store three-way mirror: fat, flabby thighs, bulging out from a bright pink bathing suit I desperately wanted to buy.

And forget the great pants that were too tight.

I knew it was time to do *something*, and that something would have to be very effective to get my thighs trim and firm fast!

In my business (creating T.V. commercials), I am in constant contact with models and celebrities who are serious about and successful at keeping their thighs thin and beautiful.

So, I embarked on a project to learn about *their* methods, talking to their doctors and beauty advisors, and then tested this program on myself and other women.

The program is (and has to be) tough, because thighs are tough to reduce. The program takes a realistic thirty days. In just one month, you *can* have thinner, firmer thighs, IF YOU WORK AT THE PROGRAM DILIGENTLY.

The THIN THIGHS IN THIRTY DAYS program has three parts: The Work-Off, The Walk-Off, and The Weight-Off. All three work together to trim your thighs, to make them sleek and sexy.

And the benefits go beyond trim thighs. You will have increased energy. You'll feel good about yourself. Exercise and careful eating will become part of your life, and everything you do will be better because of it.

Meanwhile, I'll meet you at the beach!

DOCTOR'S ENDORSEMENT

Medicine is at the dawn of self-care, and the informed consumer is now in a position to do more for her own health and appearance than ever before.

Ms. Stehling's book is a hallmark in the tradition of teaching the consumer to have a better, healthier appearance through a planned program of diet and exercise.

The energies directed toward this desired appearance offers the dividend of exercising the thighs, back, and heart muscles.

The discipline of these exercises gives you a sense of well-being and personal achievement through a better appearance and self-image.

For these reasons I recommend this book as an important addition toward improving your capacity of self-care.

Eugene McCarthy, M.D., M.P.H.
Clinical Professor Cornell University
Medical School
New York Hospital

Results

You are in for a big treat! No matter what your bone structure is, you will have firmer, more nicely shaped thighs. You can eliminate "saddle bags." You'll look sleeker in pants. Gravity pulls all the parts of your body down—everything starts to SAG. If the muscles are strong and toned, you will have fought gravity and not look bottom heavy.

The increased circulation that comes from exercise can help prevent varicose veins.

You'll find it easier to walk up stairs and do your daily errands. And you'll be able to dance all night!

Your firm thighs will feel sexy to the touch and you'll feel stronger and more attractive.

These results can only be judged in terms of appearance. Once a week use a tape measure. Measure several inches below the crotch at the same place each time. Sometimes the inches don't change drastically, but the new firm look is there.

In the beginning, although you'll be speeding up your metabolism and burning up calories, don't go by what the bathroom scale tells you. You *will be* replacing fat with firm sleek muscle by doing the exercises. However, *muscle weighs more than fat*! So, don't be discouraged if your weight stays the same. Remember, our goal is thin thighs, and we'll have them!

GET READY TO START MONDAY

First get mentally ready. The Work-Off shouldn't be viewed as a boring chore.

It's important to you because it gives you energy, beauty, and great thighs.

Diana Nyad says, **"Working out should be as basic and essential a part of your daily routine as brushing your teeth."**

Just minutes a day for 30 days.

Everyday, except Sunday, put aside some time. No excuses and no interruptions! For example, if you're tired at the end of the day, try The Work-Off and you'll feel revitalized as your circulation gets revved up. Need to wake up in the morning? The Work-Off gets you off to a fast start.

Pick a place with room enough for kicks. Exercise on a thick rug or a doubled up blanket. Don't ever exercise on the bare floor.

Wear whatever is comfortable and easy to move around in. Leotards, tee shirt and shorts, or *nothing* at all! It's a good idea to wear the same thing all the time. If you travel, take your Work-Off outfit with you.

"Diane met Sam on her daily Walk-Off; her last daily walk-off was 25 yards to the altar.

And talk about great legs on the honeymoon beach…!**"**

THE 1.
WORK-OFF

Stand in front of a mirror in your underwear. Hands on your hips. Aha! The fattest part of you is staring back—your *thighs!*

Why? Nature has given women a wide pelvic area for bearing children and chances are you have excess fat stored in this area. You can be thin everywhere else, but even with dieting you'll still be stuck with this stored fat. Specific intensive exercises are necessary.

The hip and thigh areas have large muscles. When these muscles are weak and unused, it's pretty obvious.

Periods of extended inactivity cause muscles to lose their tone. Since most of us sit most of the time (can't you just *feel* your thighs *spread?*), The Work-Off is necessary.

Those muscles must constantly work, that is, be made to contract. When they do, they become stronger and your shape looks firmer, trim.

For example, notice if you have a bulge of what appears to be fat on the inside of your lower thigh and knee. This bulge may simply be caused by a weak quadricep and muscle. Strengthen your quadriceps with exercise and the bulge should disappear.

*T*HE THIN THIGHS IN THIRTY DAY'S GOAL

It's important to have a goal firmly in your mind. Here it is: *to work* to have firmer, thinner, sexier thighs in thirty days. Nothing short of illness should keep you from your goal.

You'll devote a short time each Work-Off day to this goal. You'll never be too busy or too tired to exercise for thin thighs.

Remember, to have thin thighs, you must exercise. Learn to appreciate how good it is for you, and your efforts will pay off beautifully!

*H*OW TO DO THE WORK-OFF EXERCISES

The Work-Off is aided by concentration. These exercises mustn't be done with a "slipshod-get 'em-over-with" attitude.

Do them slowly. With control. Don't let your leg *fall. You* lower it!

Feel each exercise. What parts of your body are working? Which muscle is tight and working? Again, take it *slowly* and deliberately. Notice how your thigh muscles are being used. Concentrate!

At first your movements won't be too smooth. You should have to use considerable effort, but as soon as you get shaky and a movement gets sloppy, rest and go on to the next exercise.

You should aim to do each exercise as though it's a marvelous dance step. An audience of a thousand is watching you, amazed at how graceful you are!

That means following the instructions very carefully. These exercises shouldn't hurt your back or knees. You'll see the emphasis on a correct overall picture of your body. Your legs, hips, back, shoulders, and even your head and neck must be in proper alignment to work together in a healthful way.

Finally, RELAX! Don't hunch your shoulders. Don't be stiff. Don't frown.

Read each exercise. Twice! Learn them step-by-step. Memorize them.

There are only six exercises. Six *very* effective thigh exercises. Do them in sequence, and follow the diary. If you feel strong enough, *go ahead and do more*, if you want to!

If you can't make the goal, no problem! Everyone will go at her own pace. You do *your* best and your level of fitness will improve.

You may be a little sore. Stretch a bit and take a hot, bubbly bath; and as you soak, remember that the ache in your muscles is a signal you're making progress.

EXERCISES

A. THIGH ANGLE

Soles together

Use towel

1 *Lie on your back using a rolled towel at the base of your spine for support. Turn the soles of your feet to face each other.*

Slowly lower keeping soles together

2 *Keeping the soles together, slowly lower and bend your legs to a frog position.*

Slowly unbend legs

3 *Open your legs from the knee.*

Bring soles together

4 *Return to frog position and, keeping your soles together, raise your legs straight up to the starting position.*

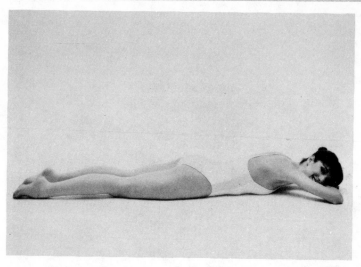

1 *Lie on your stomach, resting your head on your hands.*

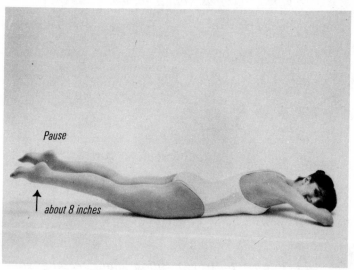

Pause

about 8 inches

2 *Raise both legs at the same time from the hips about 8 inches. Pause.*

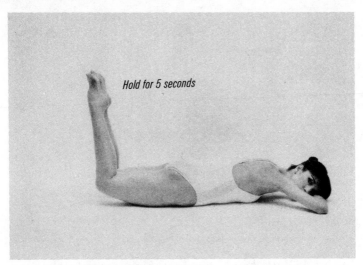

Hold for 5 seconds

3 *Bend both legs at the knees. Count 5 seconds.*

Pause

4 *Straighten legs and pause. Slowly, lower legs to start.*

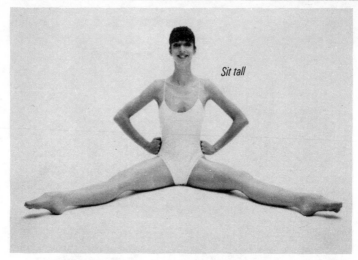

Sit tall

1 *With hands on your hips, spread your legs until you feel the tension, but not so it hurts. Keep back straight and tall.*

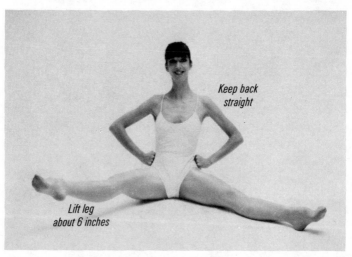

Keep back straight

Lift leg about 6 inches

2 *Lift right leg about 6 inches off the ground, but don't lean forward.*

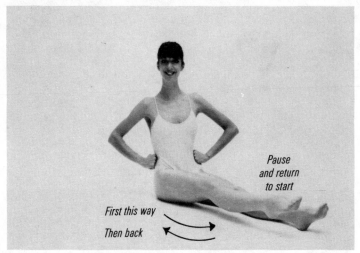

Pause
and return
to start

First this way

Then back

3 *Slowly swing your right leg to meet the left leg.
Pause, but don't drop the leg. Then still holding
the leg off the ground, return it to the starting
position and lower it. Finish right leg's count for
the day before doing the left leg.*

D. KICK KICK

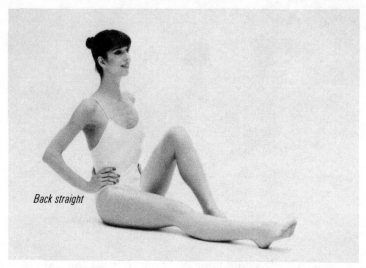

Back straight

1 *With your hands on your hips sit tall and straight. Bend your left leg.*

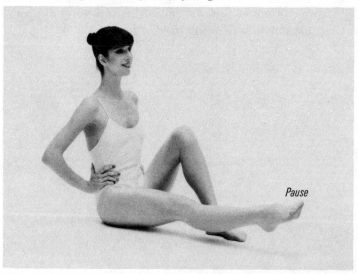

Pause

2 *Raise your right leg about 8 inches and pause.*

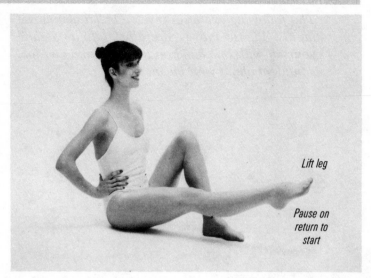

Lift leg

Pause on
return to
start

3 *Raise right leg another 8 inches and pause, keeping back straight. Lower your leg about 8 inches and pause. Then return to start. Finish right leg's daily repetition before doing the left.*

E. KICKETY SPLIT

The following exercises involve ballet-like movements. Please move carefully at first. Steady yourself with one hand on the wall until you feel confident about your balance.

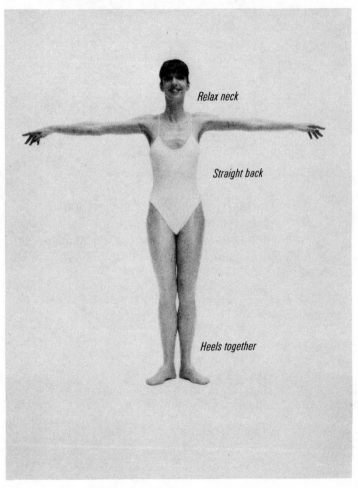

Relax neck

Straight back

Heels together

1 *Stand tall. Shoulders should be relaxed with heels together and feet turned out.*

Do these kicks gently at first. Be sure you're nice and limber. You don't want to strain a muscle or a ligament.

2 *Keeping arms steady, raise right knee to your elbow. Don't lean forward.*

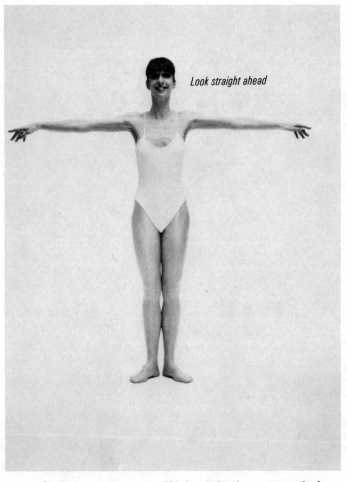

Look straight ahead

3 *Return to start. Kick right leg, extended so foot, or ankle touches your hand.*

Try to keep your leg straight. Relax your feet; you do not have to point your toes.

4 *Do full count for the right leg, then do the left leg.*

F. THIGH CHAIR

This is the toughest, most marvelous exercise for your thighs. The longer you can learn to hold this position the better.

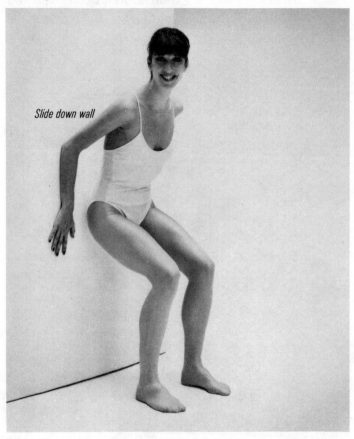

Slide down wall

1 *Stand about a foot from a wall with your feet pointing straight ahead. Slide down the wall until you are sitting with your thighs perpendicular to the wall. Rest your arms on your legs or keep them by your side. Your thighs should be level as pictured. Don't go down any lower.*

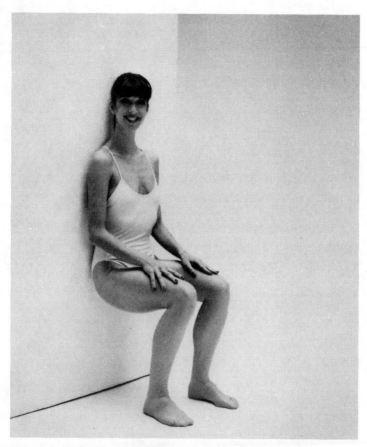

2 *As you become proficient at this exercise, you can widen the distance between your knees to make it an even more effective exercise. Also try turning your feet out.*

THE 2. WALK-OFF

Walking! Yes, this convenient *miracle* exercise can do wonders for the thighs. Yet so few women do enough (if any!) walking.

What will your daily Walk-Off do?

Well, really *walking* (as opposed to slowly window-shopping) gets you breathing harder, increasing your heart rate and circulation. Oxygen is forced into muscles and body tissues, and next thing you know those long thigh muscles start getting tighter, *noticeably* firmer.

Walking helps reduce fat and develop sexy *lean* muscle, and you will lose inches. Walk off those jiggles in your thighs.

On your daily walk you will be getting many health and beauty benefits with each step.

THE WALK-OFF CAN:

1 Lower your blood pressure and resting pulse.
2 Get your weight down.
3 Get rid of tension and anxiety.
4 Reduce headaches.
5 Help make your bones strong (especially important if you are over forty).
6 Help reduce varicose vein symptoms.
7 Give your whole body a sexy glow.
8 Help you relax—after a good walk you'll feel happier.

What about *running*? You don't have to run. Walking works just as well. It just takes more time.

Walking BURNS calories. And it lowers your appetite by influencing your appestat and keeping the blood flow from your digestive tract. At a comfortable pace (3 mph) you can walk-off a piece of pizza in about one half hour!

Figure on burning off up to 450 calories an hour —depending on your pace! You'll love to walk. You won't feel like just sitting around. You'll come to love that great feeling of exercise and fresh air.

Naturally, you may take a while (most likely about fifteen minutes!) to appreciate this wonderful daily walk, but soon it will be a thigh-thinning joy. Keep it up!

Six days a week, make time to get out and Walk-Off your thighs to thinness and firmness. I'd rather you do the *whole walk* as often as you can, but you have the option of spreading your time throughout the day. I walk to work in the morning and finish my distance by walking home at night.

Or, you can walk at lunch. Forty-five minutes later you'll *feel* thinner and the afternoon will fly by. Some women even walk around the parking lot at lunch! Get up and walk in the morning if that's easier for you. Have a nice walk at the end of the day. Do you have children? Push them in a stroller, and share babysitting with another walking mother.

Make it clear to *YOURSELF* and others you are putting aside time for *YOUR* Walk-Off.

Here are some ideas to help you enjoy your Walk-Off: Wear a head set and listen to your favorite tapes. Go on a "fantasy walk"—be a Princess, transplant yourself to a dream place, or Jane walking through the jungle! Use the walk to solve a problem. One woman I know looks for a coin each time. Another follows deer tracks on her farm.

So get away from it all. Have some fun and firm those thighs!

WHERE

Anywhere! Around the block, the shopping center (keep moving!), just step out and go. Of course, a beach or a mountain path are great, but just *walking* anywhere is refreshing, even right from your front door and around the block.

It is a good idea to pick a goal to walk to. Walk to visit friends—don't use that car!

I'll bet there's a high school near you. Go to the track, and pretend you are in the Olympics (walking is an Olympic event!). It's easy to roll off the miles on the quarter-mile track.

Anytime you can give up riding, do it! For example, get out of the golf cart. Don't pick the nearest parking spot. Pick the farthest and do your fun, thin-thigh *exercise*!

H_{OW}

Walk with good posture: don't slouch, and don't walk with your eyes to the ground. Look up and ahead, *PROUD*! Use a heel-toe action with your feet pointing forward. Relax your arms to a natural swing.

Think about how your *face* looks. Are you smiling? Frowning! Do you look relaxed? You are on your own private adventure. So *ENJOY*!

Make *every* step *count*. Really move out and feel your thighs reaching and working to firmness.

You are not on a stroll, *not* window-shopping.

When you first start out, depending on your fitness, you may feel sore and stiff. (Hey! It's working!)

If you become out of breath, slow down to rest, then try to start up again. If you get dizzy, stop. It could mean any number of things from hot weather to low blood pressure. Try again, going slower, doing less, to build yourself up. And ask your doctor.

Soon your long strides and energy will make the Walk-Off seem like floating.

It's the easiest way to thin thighs!

READY–SET–WALK-OFF!

This program is ambitious. Do the best you can. You should be able to do the time, if not the mileage, for each day. In any event, be *consistent*. Then you will see results on your thighs.

You should measure your mileage. You can do it with your car's pedometer, a measured block, or track. It feels good to see all the miles pile up, and you can see how far you are really going. If you are in an unfamiliar place, just walk your time at a brisk pace.

Ideally, you should get so that you can walk three miles in about an hour, more or less.

A reminder: Don't smoke! It has been connected to many health problems. It cuts the oxygen your legs need. It looks sloppy. It even gives you wrinkles! Smoking slows down your thin thigh program.

Now put on some comfortable, low-heeled shoes (I walk around in running shoes, carrying other shoes if I'll need them). Running shoes make walking less tiring. You feel like you're walking on a cloud. Running shoes are perfectly acceptable to wear with just about everything!

Be prepared to walk in rain or shine. If it rains, think of all the moisture your complexion is getting.

Turn to your diary. Off you go, on the road to a great pair of legs!

WALKING*

Days required to lose 5 to 25 pounds by exercise and lowering daily calorie intake

MINUTES OF WALKING	REDUCTION OF CALORIES PER DAY (IN KCAL)	DAYS TO LOSE 5 lbs.	DAYS TO LOSE 10 lbs.	DAYS TO LOSE 15 lbs.	DAYS TO LOSE 20 lbs.	DAYS TO LOSE 25 lbs.
30	400	27	54	81	108	135
30	600	20	40	60	80	100
30	800	16	32	48	64	80
30	1000	13	26	39	52	65
45	400	23	46	69	92	115
45	600	18	36	54	72	90
45	800	14	28	42	56	70
45	1000	12	24	36	48	60
60	400	21	42	63	84	105
60	600	16	32	48	64	80
60	800	13	26	39	52	65
60	1000	11	22	33	44	55

*Walking briskly (3.5-4.0 mph) calculated at 5.2 Cal/minute.

"Who says you can't wear walk-off shoes with a Valentino suit? Fitness looks great on you!"

SUIT BY VALENTINO

THE 3.
WEIGHT-OFF

Wonderful! The Work-Off and The Walk-Off are getting your thighs firm and sleek by the week!

In order to hurry things along, a little dieting for some of us may be in order!

Look in the mirror again. Are you several sizes larger than you want to be?

Maybe you've faced all this before, but now you have an incentive: you want your thighs to be in shape in thirty days!

Let's talk about motivation. You have to *want* to be thin. It is something you want so badly that you will work on it all your life. Your desire to lose weight has to be greater than your desire to reach for that box of cookies.

We often lead our lives around food: planning and preparing meals, eating in new restaurants, etc..Often we eat for many reasons when we aren't hungry. Eating can be like alcohol. Take that first bite and we're off on a binge.

Doesn't this make you unhappy? Guilt sets in and you eventually end up eating again to overcome it!

To stop overeating you need to set a goal. Set your sights on being *happy* and living a normal life. That's a big goal. If you are very overweight, working with groups like Weight Watchers or Diet Center can make this complex and frustrating behavorial problem easier to solve through the support and counsel of others. A structured diet program with a doctor, though expensive, may be right for some.

But for all of us, whether we want to lose five pounds or fifty pounds, we must make a firm, no-nonsense decision to control our eating. Take every day, one day at a time. Forget about yesterday or tomorrow. What are you putting in your mouth right now?

You have decided to do a lot of walking. You have set a time aside to exercise. So now you complete this picture of self-esteem, health, and thin thighs by tackling your eating.

The diary is a big help.

What is The Weight-Off Diet? I am not going to tell you to eat three grapefruits a day or throw raw eggs and bananas in the blender. (Ugh!)

The Weight-Off is so simple.

Calorie counting. That's it. Nothing fancy, no high-protein, gram-counting, crazy crash diets, or weird recipes.

Thirty-five hundred calories equals one pound of fat. Every 3,500 calories you eat and don't burn turns into stored fat. The trick in losing weight is in using up more calories than you eat. If you use 2,000 calories a day that's all you should eat. When dieting, eat less than you need because your body is using stored caloric energy.

Note: Remember a calorie is a calorie whether it is in lettuce or ice cream. It's just that ice cream has greater caloric density.

The number of calories you need to eat daily varies with the individual. The chart below is a rough idea:

DAILY MAINTENANCE CALORIES
If you're at your desirable weight

DESIRABLE WEIGHT	18-35 YEARS	35-55 YEARS	55-75 YEARS
99	1,700	1,500	1,300
110	1,850	1,650	1,400
121	2,000	1,750	1,550
128	2,100	1,900	1,600
132	2,150	1,950	1,650
143	2,300	2,050	1,800
154	2,400	2,150	1,850
165	2,550	2,300	1,950

"Sundays off can be fun-you can still work towards your goal

ACTIVITY AND
CALORIC REQUIREMENTS

WEIGHT	INACTIVE*	MILDLY ACTIVE**	MEDIUM ACTIVE†	ACTIVE‡	VERY ACTIVE§
95	1140	1330	1520	1710	1900
98	1176	1372	1568	1764	1960
101	1212	1414	1616	1818	2020
105	1260	1470	1680	1890	2100
110	1320	1540	1760	1980	2200
115	1380	1615	1840	2070	2300
120	1440	1680	1920	2160	2400
125	1500	1750	2000	2250	2500
130	1560	1820	2080	2340	2600
135	1620	1890	2160	2430	2700
140	1680	1960	2240	2520	2800
145	1740	2030	2320	2610	2900
150	1800	2100	2400	2700	3000
155	1860	2170	2480	2790	3100
160	1920	2240	2560	2880	3200
165	1980	2310	2640	2970	3300
175	2100	2450	2800	3150	3500
185	2220	2590	2960	3330	3700
195	2340	2730	3120	3510	3900
200	2400	2800	3200	3600	4000
210	2520	2940	3360	3780	4200
220	2640	3080	3520	3960	4400

*(Does nothing actively) Multiply your weight by 12
**(Rides to work, sits at work) Multiply your weight by 14
†(Teacher, mother of small children) Multiply your weight by 16
‡(On the move most of the time) Multiply your weight by 18
§(Physical worker plus extra exercise) Multiply your weight by 20

Just by dieting I figured that realistically, I could cut my 2,100 calorie maintenance by 500 calories a day for 35 days. (35 days x 500 calories =17,500 calories or 5 pounds.) The increased activity with The Walk-Off, though, can make it happen days *faster*.

Check with your doctor before *any* dieting. Don't go below 1,200 calories a day without a doctor's advice. Be sure you are eating nutritiously. Don't live on junkfoods. You'll lose weight and feel better eating fresh vegetables and fruits, lean meats, poultry, fish, and *low*-saturated fats.

Now go get a little notebook you can carry everywhere. Buy a small calorie counting booklet. Everyday write down what you eat and the day's total calories.

Learn to be aware of calories. A chicken breast without the skin is 320 calories, or 450 calories with the skin! A cup of sour cream is 485 calories, whereas a cup of plain yogurt (a great substitute) is 160!

HERE ARE SOME DIET TIPS:

1   Don't add salt, *ever*! Your food has plenty. Salt makes you retain water and your legs will look puffy and fat.

2   Be careful about hidden sugar. It's everywhere, even in some loaves of bread. Lots of foods you never thought of as "sweet" have sugar.

3   Watch fats, trim the meat you eat and don't pile on butter.

4   Drink eight glasses of water everday. It aids in diuresis. A glass or two before a meal may help you feel full before you eat.

5   Don't skip meals. You'll just get hungry.

6   Learn to recognize *real* hunger versus eating because you are bored, waiting for a phone call, etc.

7   Don't even buy fattening foods. Why leave a bag of potato chips around? If the rest of the household must have these foods, keep them all in a cupboard *you* never open.

8   Eat slowly. Be the last at the table to finish.

9   Feel happy if you are hungry. When you are hungry, your body is using up the fat of your body, including your thighs.

10   Never stand over the kitchen sink eating!

Losing weight takes concentration. Be prepared each day for temptations. However, don't feel depressed and guilty if you slip up. Stay positive! Use the diary!

QUESTIONS 4.
AND ANSWERS

1   QUESTION: *I have that special lumpy fat on my thighs. Is that cellulite and what can I do about it?*

ANSWER: Cellulite *isn't* some special different "woman's fat." It's plain old fat that dimples because the fat cells are distributed unevenly.

Stephen B. Kurtin, M.D., a dermatologist says, **"What we call cellulite is fat, nothing else. There are no toxins nor excess fluids floating around the fat cells."** Doctors from Johns Hopkins University studied cellulite under the microscope and found no difference between this dimply fat and other fat. Dr. David Costill, director of the Human Performance Laboratory at Ball State University in Indiana, says, **"Anatomically, fat and the condition called 'cellulite' are the same. Any dimpling is caused by uneven distribution, both in size and the amount of fat cells."**
This fat reacts to dieting and exercise.

2   QUESTION: *What ways of dressing make my thighs appear thinner?*

ANSWER: Don't wear tight jeans! Keep pants loose (not baggy) and dark-colored. Don't have your panty line showing. Don't wear "fuzzy" clothes. Wear tunic length sweaters and blouses over pants. A bikini is better than a one-piece. Eyes have a lot more to look at than your thighs!

3   QUESTION: *Does running help to thin my thighs?*

ANSWER: Yes. However, it takes a long time, more than thirty days, to become a runner. Most people can go out and *walk* several miles, but certainly not *run* them.

4   QUESTION: *I'm concerned about getting varicose veins. What should I know?*

ANSWER: You should know that inactivity and overweight contribute to the formation of varicose veins. Many walkers and runners have found their varicosity lessened, and physical activity *certainly* doesn't cause varicose veins.

DAILY DIARY

This is your day-by-day progress report. Read the rules below:

1   Start on a Monday.
2   You *must* enter every day what you've done. If it's nothing, write *nothing*.
3   Which brings us to excuses. You will accept only two: a high fever or a nuclear war.
4   This very tough program for the thighs will reflect personal fitness abilities. GOAL means the fastest results—work for the GOAL as soon as you are able. ACTUAL—good, at least you are trying and you will see results.
5   Think of the diary as an *inspirational* tool. Be proud as you see it fill up.
6   Sunday is your day off. Use this day for some fun thigh workout. Maybe go horseback riding, climb a lighthouse, play basketball with a kid—go to the Y and swim—enjoy!
7   Have fun. Each day you will be more beautiful, lucky hard working you!

Please see instructions on the previous page.

1st MONDAY

	WORK-OFF	GOAL	ACTUAL
	Exercise A	5	
	B	3	
	C	2	
	D	3	
	E	3	
	F	2x5 sec.	
THE WALK-OFF	Miles	½	
	Time	15 min.	
THE WEIGHT-OFF	Calories Today		

1st TUESDAY

	WORK-OFF	GOAL	ACTUAL
	Exercise A	7	
	B	3	
	C	2	
	D	3	
	E	3	
	F	2x5 sec.	
THE WALK-OFF	Miles	½	
	Time	15 min.	
THE WEIGHT-OFF	Calories Today		

1st WEDNESDAY

	WORK-OFF	GOAL	ACTUAL
	Exercise A	8	
	B	3	
	C	2	
	D	3	
	E	4	
	F	2x5 sec.	
THE WALK-OFF	Miles	¾	
	Time	15 min.	
THE WEIGHT-OFF	Calories Today		

Note: If you are already active and the first day seems quite easy, double the next eight days' assignments.

1st THURSDAY

	WORK-OFF	GOAL	ACTUAL
	Exercise A	9	
	B	3	
	C	3	
	D	3	
	E	5	
	F	3x5 sec.	
THE WALK-OFF	Miles	¾	
	Time	15 min.	
THE WEIGHT-OFF	Calories Today		

1st FRIDAY

	WORK-OFF	GOAL	ACTUAL
	Exercise A	10	
	B	4	
	C	3	
	D	4	
	E	2x3	
	F	2x5 sec.	
THE WALK-OFF	Miles	¾	
	Time	15 min.	
THE WEIGHT-OFF	Calories Today		

1st SATURDAY

	WORK-OFF	GOAL	ACTUAL
	Exercise A	10	
	B	5	
	C	4	
	D	2x3	
	E	2x3	
	F	3x5 sec.	
THE WALK-OFF	Miles	1	
	Time	20 min.	
THE WEIGHT-OFF	Calories Today		

1st SUNDAY

2nd MONDAY

WORK-OFF	GOAL	ACTUAL
Exercise A	10	
B	6	
C	5	
D	2x3	
E	2x3	
F	3x5 sec.	
THE WALK-OFF Miles	1	
Time	15 min.	
THE WEIGHT-OFF Calories Today		

2nd TUESDAY

WORK-OFF	GOAL	ACTUAL
Exercise A	20	
B	12	
C	2x5	
D	2x6	
E	2x6	
F	3x10 sec.	
THE WALK-OFF Miles	2	
Time	35 min.	
THE WEIGHT-OFF Calories Today		

2nd WEDNESDAY

WORK-OFF	GOAL	ACTUAL
Exercise A	20	
B	7	
C	2x5	
D	2x6	
E	2x6	
F	3x10 sec.	
THE WALK-OFF Miles	2	
Time	35 min.	
THE WEIGHT-OFF Calories Today		

2nd THURSDAY

	WORK-OFF	GOAL	ACTUAL
Exercise A		20	
B		7	
C		2x6	
D		2x6	
E		2x6	
F		3x15 sec.	
THE WALK-OFF	Miles	2	
	Time	35 min.	
THE WEIGHT-OFF	Calories Today		

2nd FRIDAY

	WORK-OFF	GOAL	ACTUAL
Exercise A		20	
B		8	
C		2x7	
D		2x6	
E		2x7	
F		3x15 sec.	
THE WALK-OFF	Miles	2	
	Time	35 min.	
THE WEIGHT-OFF	Calories Today		

2nd SATURDAY

	WORK-OFF	GOAL	ACTUAL
Exercise A		20	
B		8	
C		2x7	
D		2x7	
E		2x7	
F		3x15 sec.	
THE WALK-OFF	Miles	3+	
	Time	60 min.	
THE WEIGHT-OFF	Calories Today		

2nd SUNDAY

3rd MONDAY

	WORK-OFF	GOAL	ACTUAL
Exercise	A	20	
	B	10	
	C	2x8	
	D	2x8	
	E	2x8	
	F	2x30 sec.	
THE WALK-OFF	Miles	1½	
	Time	30 min.	
THE WEIGHT-OFF	Calories Today		

3rd TUESDAY

	WORK-OFF	GOAL	ACTUAL
Exercise	A	30	
	B	10	
	C	2x8	
	D	2x8	
	E	2x8	
	F	2x30 sec.	
THE WALK-OFF	Miles	2	
	Time	35 min.	
THE WEIGHT-OFF	Calories Today		

3rd WEDNESDAY

	WORK-OFF	GOAL	ACTUAL
Exercise	A	30	
	B	10	
	C	2x8	
	D	2x8	
	E	2x8	
	F	2x30 sec.	
THE WALK-OFF	Miles	2	
	Time	35 min.	
THE WEIGHT-OFF	Calories Today		

3rd THURSDAY

	WORK-OFF	GOAL	ACTUAL
	Exercise A	30	_____
	B	10	_____
	C	2x8	_____
	D	2x8	_____
	E	2x10	_____
	F	2x30 sec.	_____
THE WALK-OFF	Miles	2	_____
	Time	35 min.	_____
THE WEIGHT-OFF	Calories Today	_____	_____

3rd FRIDAY

	WORK-OFF	GOAL	ACTUAL
	Exercise A	30	_____
	B	10	_____
	C	2x0	_____
	D	2x8	_____
	E	2x10	_____
	F	2x30 sec.	_____
THE WALK-OFF	Miles	2¼	_____
	Time	40 min.	_____
THE WEIGHT-OFF	Calories Today	_____	_____

3rd SATURDAY

	WORK-OFF	GOAL	ACTUAL
	Exercise A	30	_____
	B	10	_____
	C	2x10	_____
	D	2x8	_____
	E	2x10	_____
	F	3x30 sec.	_____
THE WALK-OFF	Miles	3+	_____
	Time	60 min.	_____
THE WEIGHT-OFF	Calories Today	_____	_____

3rd SUNDAY

4th MONDAY

	WORK-OFF	GOAL	ACTUAL
	Exercise A	30	
	B	10	
	C	2x10	
	D	2x8	
	E	2x10	
	F	3x30 sec.	
THE WALK-OFF	Miles	2½	
	Time	45 min.	
THE WEIGHT-OFF	Calories Today		

4th TUESDAY

	WORK-OFF	GOAL	ACTUAL
	Exercise A	30	
	B	10	
	C	2x10	
	D	2x8	
	E	2x10	
	F	3x30 sec.	
THE WALK-OFF	Miles	2½	
	Time	45 min.	
THE WEIGHT-OFF	Calories Today		

4th WEDNESDAY

	WORK-OFF	GOAL	ACTUAL
	Exercise A	30	
	B	10	
	C	2x10	
	D	2x8	
	E	2x10	
	F	3x30 sec.	
THE WALK-OFF	Miles	2½	
	Time	45 min.	
THE WEIGHT-OFF	Calories Today		

4th THURSDAY

WORK-OFF	GOAL	ACTUAL
Exercise A	30	_____
B	10	_____
C	2x10	_____
D	2x8	_____
E	2x10	_____
F	3x30 sec.	_____
THE WALK-OFF Miles	2½	_____
Time	45 min.	_____
THE WEIGHT-OFF Calories Today	_____	_____

4th FRIDAY

WORK-OFF	GOAL	ACTUAL
Exercise A	30	_____
B	10	_____
C	2x10	_____
D	2x8	_____
E	2x10	_____
F	3x30 sec.	_____
THE WALK-OFF Miles	2½	_____
Time	45 min.	_____
THE WEIGHT-OFF Calories Today	_____	_____

4th SATURDAY

WORK-OFF	GOAL	ACTUAL
Exercise A	30	_____
B	10	_____
C	2x10	_____
D	2x8	_____
E	2x10	_____
F	3x30 sec.	_____
THE WALK-OFF Miles	3+	_____
Time	60 min.	_____
THE WEIGHT-OFF Calories Today	_____	_____

4th SUNDAY

5th MONDAY

WORK-OFF	GOAL	ACTUAL
Exercise A	30	_____
B	10	_____
C	2x10	_____
D	2x8	_____
E	2x10	_____
F	3x30 sec.	_____
THE WALK-OFF Miles	2½	_____
Time	45 min.	_____
THE WEIGHT-OFF Calories Today	_____	_____

5th TUESDAY

WORK-OFF	GOAL	ACTUAL
Exercise A	30	_____
B	10	_____
C	2x10	_____
D	2x8	_____
E	2x10	_____
F	3x30 sec.	_____
THE WALK-OFF Miles	2½	_____
Time	45 min.	_____
THE WEIGHT-OFF Calories Today	_____	_____

You did it! Now keep up the good work. With regular exercise and by watching your diet you'll really stay trim.

REFERENCES

1 Chaback, Elaine, THE COMPLETE CALORIE COUNTER, Dell 1979

2 Cooper, Kenneth and Mildred, AEROBICS FOR WOMEN, M. Evans 1972

3 Dugan, Ann, THE WOMAN'S "NO SWEAT" EXERCISE BOOK, Fawcett 1981

4 Eisen, Gail, Friedman, Philip, THE PILATES METHOD OF PHYSICAL AND MENTAL CONDITIONING, Warner 1981

5 Pearlman, Barbara, SLENDERCISES, Doubleday

6 Pritikin, Nathan, THE PRITIKIN PROGRAM FOR DIET AND EXERCISE, Bantam 1980

7 Stutman, Fred, M.D. THE DOCTOR'S WALKING BOOK, Ballantine 1980

8 Westin, Jeane, THE THIN BOOK, Comp Care 1978

9 COUNT CALORIES, CALORIES COUNT! David McKay Co.

ABOUT THE AUTHOR

Wendy Stehling, an executive at a large New York advertising agency, is originally from Chevy Chase, Maryland. She lives near Central Park where she likes to do her daily morning Walk-off.